TIM
TO THE
LIGHTHOUSE

Edward Ardizzone

To Jasper.
Happy Christmas 1989
Lots of love Becky xxx

OXFORD UNIVERSITY PRESS
Oxford   New York   Toronto

Oxford University Press, Walton Street, Oxford OX2 6DP

Oxford   New York   Toronto
Delhi   Bombay   Calcutta   Madras   Karachi
Petaling Jaya   Singapore   Hong Kong   Tokyo
Nairobi   Dar es Salaam   Cape Town
Melbourne   Auckland

and associated companies in
Berlin   Ibadan

Oxford is a trade mark of Oxford University Press

© Edward Ardizzone 1968

First published 1968
Reprinted 1979, 1980
First published in this reset edition 1989

*To my cousin Christianna Brand
and to my tenth grandchild
Jessica*

Printed in Hong Kong

Tim and his parents and his friends
Charlotte and Ginger lived in a house by the
sea.

Often the children would play on the beach
and would talk to the old boatman who was
always kind to them.

Sometimes, when the day was fine and the sea calm, he would take them out to the lighthouse.

The lighthouse keeper was a friend of theirs. He always saw them coming and was on the little stone jetty below the lighthouse to help them out of the boat.

'Have you anything for me?' he would
say to the boatman.

The boatman usually had. Sometimes it
was a parcel from the keeper's wife or a letter

from his youngest daughter who had just learnt to read and write.

'Ah!' he would say. 'I wish they were here. It is lonely sometimes with just me and Ernie, my mate, though he is a good lad and handy with his work.'

The keeper sometimes let the children explore the lighthouse.

In the bottom room were a few hens. The keeper liked an egg for his breakfast.

The room above was a store-room and the one above that an engine room in which electricity was made for the light.

Above that again was a bedroom and then a kitchen, and right on top in the highest room of all was the light itself.

And all the rooms were round.

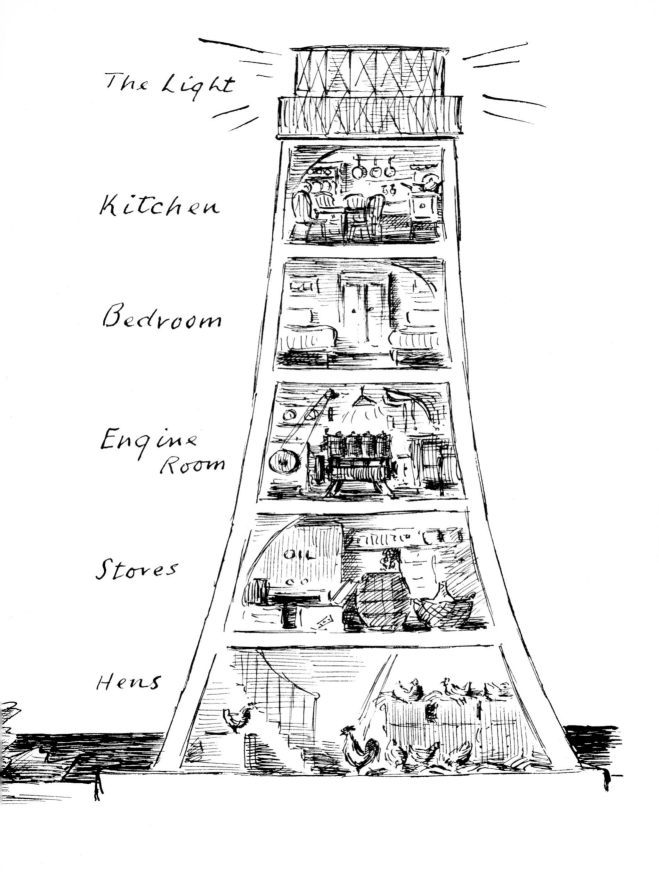

The Light

Kitchen

Bedroom

Engine Room

Stores

Hens

When there was a parcel for Ernie, Charlotte
would dash ahead, climbing the winding stairs,
looking in all the rooms, until she found him.

He was usually at the top, polishing the
bright glass of the light.

Ernie was her favourite.

Many a time they would stay for tea, and while they were eating their bread and jam, the keeper would tell them tales of terrible storms, when for weeks on end no boat from the shore could reach them.

Charlotte always felt how strange it was to eat one's tea in a round room.

At night, when Tim was at home, before he got into bed, he would draw back the curtains of his window.

Then, once every minute, the great beam of light from the lighthouse would shine into his room.

It made him happy to see it because he knew that ships far out to sea could see it too, and so steer clear of the dangerous rocks at its base.

Often he would lie half asleep in his bed wishing and wishing he could be a lighthouse keeper.

One night, and it was a stormy one, Tim was woken by the noise of the wind rattling the window frames and the sound of waves crashing on the beach.

He waited for the beam of light to shine into the room. It never came.

He waited and waited but still no light. So he realized that something terrible had happened. The light of the lighthouse was out, and ships that passed in the night might be wrecked on the dangerous rocks.

Tim was worried, so he went to wake his father. 'Drat the boy!' said his father. 'Go back to bed Tim, and stop your nonsense.'

But once back in bed Tim could not sleep. He lay awake and worried more than ever.

At last he could bear it no longer. He got up, pulled his rubber boots on over his pyjama trousers, put on his red jersey, his raincoat and mackintosh hat and set out to find his old friend Captain McFee.

When Tim arrived at Captain McFee's house he banged on the door.

The old man put his head out of a window.

'The light from the lighthouse is out,' Tim called up to him.

For a moment or two the Captain said nothing, and then he said suddenly, 'Why bless my soul! You are right, my boy. Come in and I will phone the coastguard station.'

But the gale had blown down the telephone lines and he could not get through.

'There is only one thing to do,' said the Captain. 'We must take my boat and go out to the lighthouse and see what has happened. Though it may be a dangerous voyage.'

Now, what Tim did not know was that Charlotte and Ginger had followed him out of the house and at this very moment were hiding behind Captain McFee's hedge.

There they heard everything that Tim and the Captain had said.

Of course they wanted to go to the lighthouse too, but knew that if they asked the Captain he was bound to say 'NO'. So they slipped quietly ahead and hid in the boat before Tim and the Captain arrived.

Tim helped the Captain to push the boat down the steep shingle beach into the sea.

The night was dark. The sea was rough and the voyage was dangerous.

Captain McFee made Tim steer the boat, because he knew that Tim's young eyes could see better than his own, which were dim with age.

When they were well out to sea Charlotte and Ginger came out of their hiding-place.

Captain McFee seemed terribly cross, but he said to himself, 'Oh well, they might be useful.' And so they were.

After what seemed a long time, Tim's sharp

eyes spotted the little stone jetty.

Soon they were alongside and had scrambled out of the boat and into the lighthouse.

There, in the lowest room, they found the lighthouse keeper. He was lying on the floor among his hens. He was tied up with ropes and was unconscious.

They untied his ropes and made him as comfortable as possible; then they left him and went in search of Ernie.

They found him in the top room. He too was bound up and unconscious. Also he was bleeding from a nasty wound on the head.

Oh! Poor Ernie

Quickly they untied his ropes, and Charlotte bathed his head.

Ernie opened his eyes for a moment and said in a faint voice, 'Wreckers! Switches – top row – third from right – bottom row – second from left – fuse switch – handle.' Then he shut his eyes and was unconscious once more.

Tim, who had been listening carefully, rushed to the switchboard and pulled all the right switches and the handle.

At once a great light beamed out and started to turn slowly round.

The lighthouse was working again.

'Bravo, Tim!' said the Captain. 'But wreckers! I don't like the sound of it. They are evil
men and may come back to turn out the light
again.'

Then he pointed to another bright light
which was shining far away on the distant
shore.

That light, he told Tim, was a false one.

A great ship was due to pass by soon and the wreckers hoped that if the lighthouse light was out, the ship would follow the false one and so get dashed to pieces on the rocks below.

The wreckers would then be able to steal any rich cargo that was washed ashore by the angry sea.

'Oh!' said Ginger. 'I'm so frightened.'

'But you must be brave Ginger, my boy,' said the Captain. 'Because I want you to take the boat and sail it alone to the coastguard station on the shore and tell the guards to come and help us.'

'Hurry now, our lives depend on it.'

Then he told Tim to guard the light and Charlotte to look after Ernie while he himself went downstairs to bar the door and attend to the lighthouse keeper.

They all felt happier when they heard the spluttering sound of the engine of the Captain's

boat, and knew that Ginger was on his way
for help.

Alone and high up in the top room of
the lighthouse, Tim and Charlotte spoke in
whispers.

Sometimes Tim would polish the glass of

the light as he had seen Ernie do, while Charlotte sat by Ernie and watched over him.

Time went slowly by. They felt they had been there for hours when suddenly there was a terrible noise of banging, crashing and shouting. Then came a rush of feet on the stairs and two rough men burst into the room.

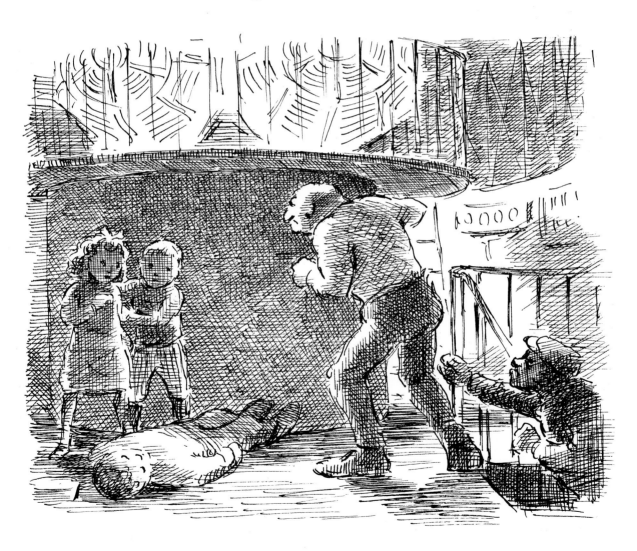

One man went to the switchboard and tried to turn out the light. But nothing happened. He had forgotten which switches were the right ones.

Then he picked up Tim, shook him roughly and said, 'Tell me what to do, you little wretch, or I will make mincemeat of you.'

'Don't tell him! Don't tell him!' shouted Charlotte, and Tim said, 'No, I won't.'

It was very brave of Tim to say no, because he was frightened and did not want to be made into mincemeat.

But at that moment, out of the corner of his eye, he caught sight of the great ship gliding past, It was all lit up and he could

just hear the music of the band playing in the first-class lounge.

'You are too late,' said Tim to the man. 'Look out there, the ship has passed us.'

The man turned to look and then with a cry of 'Foiled again' and with a fearful oath he threw Tim to the ground.

'Come on mate,' he shouted to his companion. 'Let's get out of here before the coastguards arrive!'

But the evil men were too late even for this. There was a sound of many boots on the stairs and in burst Ginger, looking terribly brave, and close behind him were the coastguards.

There was a tremendous battle. The wreckers, being desperate villains, fought like tigers, and it was a long time before the coastguards could overpower them and lead them away.

Many of the coastguards were slightly hurt,
so Charlotte was busier than ever bathing
black eyes and bandaging cuts.

Now you may be wondering what had happened to Captain McFee all this time.

He had tried to stop the wreckers coming into the lighthouse. They had knocked him on the head with a heavy stick and he now lay unconscious on the floor beside the lighthouse keeper in the lower room.

The head coastguard told two of his guards

to stay behind and look after the light and feed the hens.

Then the rest gently lifted the three unconscious men on to stretchers and carried them down to the coastguard launch.

Tim, Charlotte and Ginger followed them. They felt very happy but very, very tired.

Soon they were all stowed safely on board.
The two wreckers were chained up so they
could not escape.

It was dawn. The sea by now was calm and

the little waves sparkled in the morning light.

By the time they reached the shore, Tim, Charlotte and Ginger were fast asleep.

When they arrived at the pier Tim and

Ginger woke up, but Charlotte was so fast asleep that she had to be carried on shore.

Captain McFee, the lighthouse keeper and Ernie were carried to the hospital. They were still unconscious.

The two wreckers scowled horribly as they were led off to prison by the police.

Tim's mother and father were there to take Tim, Charlotte and Ginger home.

Once at home the children went happily to bed. They were so tired that they slept and slept and slept.

When they woke up they were surprised to find that they were now quite famous. Everybody knew how brave they and Captain McFee had been.

Ginger, as always, had to boast about it.

Captain McFee and the lighthouse keeper were soon better and were allowed to go

home, though the Captain was rather shaky and had to stay indoors for a bit.

Ernie, who had a really nasty head wound, was kept in hospital for some time longer.

Charlotte would visit him every day and sit and read to him.

He liked this very much.

Though I must admit that sometimes, when
Charlotte found Ernie's girl friend with him,
she could not help feeling a tiny bit jealous.

THE END